The No-Nonsense Key

Read the NO-NONSENSE FINANCIAL GUIDE TO UNDERSTANDING MUTUAL FUNDS

- if you have $250 or more and want to invest wisely
- if you want a potentially high investment
- if you want an investment that is easy to understand and easy to follow

Look for these other titles in the NO-NONSENSE FINANCIAL GUIDE series:

NO-NONSENSE FINANCIAL GUIDE TO UNDERSTANDING COMMON STOCKS

NO-NONSENSE FINANCIAL GUIDE TO UNDERSTANDING IRAS

NO-NONSENSE FINANCIAL GUIDE TO UNDERSTANDING MONEY MARKET FUNDS

NO-NONSENSE FINANCIAL GUIDE TO UNDERSTANDING THE STOCK MARKET

No-Nonsense Financial Guide to Understanding
Mutual Funds

Arnold Corrigan and Phyllis C. Kaufman

Longmeadow Press

To Harry & Gertrude Kaufman, with Love

This publication is designed to provide accurate and authoritative information with regard to the subject matter covered. It is sold with the understanding that neither the publisher nor the authors are engaged in rendering legal, accounting, or other professional service regarding the subject matter covered. If legal advice or other expert assistance is desired, the services of a competent professional person should be sought.

The NO-NONSENSE FINANCIAL GUIDE Series was designed and produced exclusively for, and is published exclusively by, Longmeadow Press, an imprint of Waldenbooks®. For information address: Waldenbooks Co., Inc., 201 High Ridge Rd., Stamford, Connecticut 06904.

ISBN: 0-681-29916-9

Production services: W. S. Konecky Associates
Text and cover design: Adrian Taylor

Printed in the United States of America

CONTENTS

Preface

Your financial security and that of your family depend on making the most of your money now. With as little as $250 or $500 to invest, the NO-NONSENSE FINANCIAL GUIDES will introduce you, step by step, into the world of finance.

The NO-NONSENSE FINANCIAL GUIDES put you in control.

The NO-NONSENSE FINANCIAL GUIDES take the fear out of finance.

Geared toward your financial goals, each easy-to-follow book in the NO-NONSENSE series introduces you into a different part of the world of investment opportunity.

Read several NO-NONSENSE FINANCIAL GUIDES before you invest. The short time it takes you to read and understand a NO-NONSENSE FINANCIAL GUIDE is your first step toward a secure future.

Chapter One

Introduction: Who Should Read the NO-NONSENSE FINANCIAL GUIDE TO UNDERSTANDING MUTUAL FUNDS

If you have a million dollars to invest, or even half a million, you will be welcomed at any investment advisory firm or bank trust department. You will be offered the best investment advice money can buy. However, if you have considerably less money to invest, say only $250 or $500, and you realize that intelligent financial planning is essential for your security and that of your family, finding an expert whom you can trust and who will have the time to devote to your account is not easy. Fortunately, there is a nearly perfect answer to this dilemma. The answer is *mutual funds.*

In a mutual fund, many small and some not so small investors *pool* their money into a large fund organized and managed by professionals. Each investor owns shares in the pool, according to the amount contributed. So, even if you have only $250 or $500 to invest, don't despair—you are rich enough to afford the best investment advice in town.

Chapter Two
What Are Your Investment Goals?

To get the most out of a mutual fund—or anything else—you need to be clear about what you are trying to accomplish. Since your future comfort may depend on how wisely you invest your savings, you owe it to yourself to think through your goals carefully.

Making Your Money Grow

Years ago, most Americans were content to leave their savings in a bank of some sort and to accept whatever rate of interest the bank paid. If they didn't need to spend the interest every year, they left it in the bank so that their money would grow. But habits and opportunities have changed. People have become aware that there are other ways of investing—real estate and common stocks, for example—that can make money grow more rapidly.

Moreover, we are living in an inflationary world. The *real* value of your dollars shrinks every year. If you don't find a way to increase the number of dollars you own, you automatically fall behind.

Investment Risks and Rewards

Investing also involves a trade-off between *risk* and *reward*. The higher the reward you aim for, the greater the risks are likely to be. If you invest for maximum growth, the risks will probably be substantial. But even if you aim simply at higher-than-average income, you will almost certainly take some risks that you should be aware of.

Is it a mistake to take any risks? Not at all. Risk is a part of life, just as it is a part of investing. Sometimes there are risks in choices we regard as safe. Money left in a savings bank may seem perfectly secure, yet inflation may eat away the value of the money every year. The risk is hidden but it's there. Great opportunities may be wasted by refusing to take reasonable, moderate risks. In investing, as elsewhere, you should be clear as to what the risks are, keep them as limited as you can, and make sure that the risks are reasonable in relation to what you are trying to accomplish.

Mutual Funds—a Reasonable Risk Investment

What has all this to do with mutual funds? Mutual funds have

How the Purchasing Power of the Dollar Has Shrunk
(20 years, Dec. 1963 – Dec. 1983)

	Annual Shrinkage (%)*	Real Value of Dollar
1963		$1.00
1964	1.2%	.99
1965	1.9	.97
1966	3.4	.94
1967	3.0	.91
1968	4.7	.87
1969	6.1	.82
1970	5.5	.78
1971	3.4	.75
1972	3.4	.73
1973	8.8	.67
1974	12.2	.60
1975	7.0	.56
1976	4.8	.53
1977	6.8	.50
1978	9.0	.46
1979	13.3	.40
1980	12.4	.36
1981	8.9	.33
1982	3.9	.32
1983	3.8	.30

*Annual change in Consumer Price Index

features that tend to keep your risks down. They certainly don't eliminate risk—that shouldn't be expected—but they are a remarkably good way of keeping your risks down to reasonable levels in relation to your investment objectives.

In addition, you will be able to find, among the many mutual funds available, several that are geared toward specific investment goals and the degree of risk that you feel comfortable in taking.

Chapter Three

The Real Distinction Between Growth and Income

Mutual funds, and most other investments, are generally classified as being primarily for "growth" or primarily for "income." At first glance, the distinction seems clear: in a "growth" investment, the number of your dollars, or the amount of your investment, will (you hope) increase over time, while, in an "income" investment, current spendable money will be generated. But actually, the real difference is not that simple.

In some investments, there's a very clear line between growth and income. If you buy a house for $50,000, and rent it out to other people for $5,000 a year, then the $5,000 a year is your *income* from the investment (setting aside for the moment any taxes and other expenses you may have).

If, at the end of three years, the market value of the house has risen to $60,000, then you have had *growth* of $10,000 in the value of your investment (or a 20% increase in the original $50,000).

But in many investments, the distinction may be less clear. For instance, bank accounts and money market funds are thought of as pure *income* investments because you know that the number of dollars you put into these accounts will remain absolutely fixed and will earn regular *interest* or *dividends* that could be currently spendable. Still, if you don't need to spend this interest or dividends, you may choose to leave them in the account as a way of *making your money grow.*

It can also work the other way. Let's say that five years ago you bought shares of a "growth" mutual fund for $5,000. The fund has been successful, and while you have little or no *income* (as dividends) from the investment, the shares are now worth $10,000. This year you badly need extra money to spend. So you take $1,000 out of the account and leave $9,000 in. Thus this "growth" fund has also provided you with needed "income."

Inflation makes the whole situation more complicated. Inflation has been a serious problem in the United States since the mid-1960s, and no one expects the problem to go away in the near future. Because of inflation, every dollar you own is worth less in real terms every year. In the example of the bank account or money market fund we mentioned above, you may decide that you have to let your interest or dividends (your "income") accumulate in the account simply to keep the *real value* of your investment from shrinking because of inflation.

So the line between the traditional definition of "income" and "growth" may not always be clear, and the words may not always mean exactly what you think they mean. Let's talk instead about two very clear choices that you will have to make in planning and handling your investments.

The first choice is quite straightforward. To get away from the words "income" and "growth" let's say that the choice is between *spending* money from your investment account and *letting it accumulate.* If you are trying to protect your financial future in an inflationary world, the obvious choice is to spend only what you absolutely need and to let as much as you can accumulate.

The second choice involves more thought on your part because it involves the degree of risk you are willing to take. What generally distinguishes the so-called income investments is that they are *lower-risk.* The value of your original investment—your "principal"—either holds absolutely constant (as in the bank account or money market fund) or is expected to fluctuate only moderately, while a relatively predictable amount of "income" is added to the account every year in the form of interest or dividends. The investment is *lower-risk* because its rewards are *more predictable.*

What is a "growth" investment? It may be a piece of property in a newly developing neighborhood, or a painting that you think will rise in value, or a share in a business that is growing rapidly. A "growth" mutual fund is a common stock fund that invests in shares of businesses that it thinks will rise in value substantially. Because there is no guarantee that this will happen and because the results are much less predictable, the *risks* in these investments are higher. If the investment is unsuccessful, its value may decline rather than grow, and even the growth investments that are most successful over the long term may fluctuate in value from year to year, often sharply. But many investors are willing to take these risks because *the best "growth" investments have built up people's money much faster than the best "income" investments.*

There are many mutual funds with outstanding growth records over periods of 15 or 20 years or more. They have proved their ability. They can be unpredictable and they do carry risk, but substantially less risk than most nonfund types of growth investments. They are well worth considering by anyone who is planning investments over the long term.

But if you are only comfortable with lower levels of fluctuation and more predictability, there are mutual funds for you too. We will say more about the different types of mutual funds below. But first let us explore some of the advantages that have made mutual funds such a popular type of investment.

Chapter Four

Advantages of Mutual Funds

Professional Management

Let's backtrack for a moment. At the very beginning of this book, we pointed out that the mutual funds let even the small investor enjoy the best investment advice in town. With fund sizes ranging from a few million to several billion dollars, the funds can afford to hire the best managers in the world (called "portfolio managers" because the fund's collection of securities is its "portfolio").

Are fund managers really that good?

The answer is yes and no. Investment management is still more of an art than a science, and the professional managers, who are only human beings, range from exceptionally good to pretty poor. You have to know how to study the record and pick a good-quality fund (see Chapter 10) or you need to deal with a broker or salesperson who is knowledgeable and honest enough to help you choose.

How much difference does a good manager make? A big difference. Even in a money market fund, where the range of securities that can be bought is quite limited, a good manager will have an edge over a mediocre one. In common stock funds—by far the most popular and important type of fund after the money market funds—the problems of choice multiply. In the common stock funds there are major differences in results among different managers, and the gap between the best-performing and worst-performing funds is very wide. But the best-performing common stock funds have made their shareholders' money grow, over the long term, at rates as much as 10% *above* the rate of inflation. Of course, the investment quality and performance of a mutual fund depends upon more than the skill of one or two portfolio managers. The funds have their own research staffs, and access to professional research and advisory services that are simply beyond reach of the average investor. And they work at it full time.

Diversification

In addition to professional management, a mutual fund gives you a second advantage that is important—that of *diversification.*

Diversification is another *advantage of scale*—an advantage, like that of professional management, arising from having your money pooled with that of thousands of other investors to create a fund that may amount to $50 or $100 million or more. With that amount of money available, the professional managers are able to spread the fund's investments over as many as 100 or 150 different securities. If any one of these securities goes sour, the effect on the fund is relatively small. On the other hand, if you are a do-it-yourself investor with your money concentrated in perhaps five or ten stocks and/or bonds, a disaster in any one of them will cut deeply into your total results. Diversification is an important advantage of scale because it *reduces risk*.

Note that the fund managers don't haphazardly buy many individual securities. They try to strike a very careful balance among different *types* of securities in the portfolio, so that the fund won't run the risk of having all its investments weighted in a single direction. In a common stock fund, the investments are likely to be diversified across a large number of different industries. In a bond fund, the managers might strike a balance between very long-term bonds (that is, bonds that won't come due for 20 or 30 years) and some intermediate-term or shorter-term bonds.

In theory, of course, you could diversify by buying many different securities for yourself. But this takes both knowledge and time. And because you would be buying and selling securities in small dollar amounts, you would find your transaction costs (primarily brokerage commissions) relatively high—perhaps distressingly high.

Quantity Trading

A fund has other *advantages of scale* because it buys and sells securities in large quantities. These include:

(a) *Lower commissions:* Because the average fund trades in large quantities, the brokerage commission rates it pays when buying or selling stocks, bonds or other securities are only a fraction of the commission rates paid by a small investor.

(b) *Buying Power:* Quantity trading may also occasionally give a fund better buying or selling prices. And there are certain securities that can only be bought efficiently in large quantities—like certain bond issues that are typically traded in lots of $100,000 or more. Or consider U.S. Treasury bonds, which generally sell in units of at least $10,000, with the best prices available on trades of $1 million or higher.

Chapter Five

More Advantages of Mutual Funds

There are other advantages of mutual funds that aren't direct advantages of scale, but that contribute to the usefulness and popularity of the funds. Among these are:

1. Liquidity.
2. Switching arrangements.
3. Convenience features and service.
4. Simplified retirement plans.
5. The goldfish bowl effect.
6. Simplified accounting.

Liquidity

Liquidity means that you can put your money in an investme and take it out easily, quickly and without penalty. A "liquid investment"—one with high liquidity—is an investment that i easily bought or sold.

Mutual funds are highly liquid investments. Every mutual fund will buy back ("redeem") its shares on any business day at net asset value. (The concept of "net asset value" is discusse in Chapter 9.)

There is no minimum holding time—you are free to sell o the check for your purchase has cleared. By law, the fund mus pay you your money within seven days of the redemption date The net asset value may be more or less than your original co depending on how the fund has performed, but you don't hav to worry about whether there is a buyer in the market for you stock.

Switching

If your fund is part of a larger group with several different ty of funds, you will usually be offered simplified arrangements for switching from one fund to another, should investment co ditions or your goals change. Switching by telephone has bec common, either at no cost or for a nominal fee. Many investo use this privilege for switching between money market funds and common stock funds. (See Chapter 18.)

Convenience and Service

Convenience and service are among the prime attractions that have helped the mutual funds grow. Your shares are generally held by the fund's shareholder servicing agent (a bank or other organization), so that you do not need to be bothered with safe-keeping of certificates. (In industry terminology, you have an "open account," and you are credited with owning "unissued shares," or "bookshares.") At least once a year, the agent sends you statements showing your transactions and the number of shares in your account. You can arrange to have the dividends automatically reinvested. All funds have simplified procedures for you to add money to your account whenever you wish; many have automatic investment plans under which you can authorize your own bank to send regular amounts to the fund for investment. And when you are ready to take money out, most funds offer automatic withdrawal plans under which shares are automatically redeemed to provide you with regular monthly or quarterly checks planned to meet your cash needs. Most funds have toll-free ("800") numbers, and if you need help in using these services, the people who answer the phones are surprisingly good and helpful at giving you the advice you need.

Simplified Retirement Plans

Most mutual funds offer simplified retirement plans, making it easy to invest your plan money for the long term, with all earnings plowed back into the account. The most popular plan, of course, is the IRA (Individual Retirement Account), which is open to almost everyone who works for a living (see Chapter 21, and the NO-NONSENSE FINANCIAL GUIDE TO IRAS, for more information). The IRA plans offered by the funds meet all tax law requirements. Most funds also have their own self-employed retirement plans ("Keogh" plans), approved by the IRS. Various other types of retirement plans also are offered by many funds.

The "Goldfish Bowl" Effect

The people who run mutual funds operate in a "goldfish bowl." On any given day, you can pick up the financial section of the newspaper and find out how your fund is doing. (To learn how to read the newspaper quotations, turn to Chapter 13.) You can also track your fund's performance and compare it to other funds through publications that analyze performance over periods ranging from one week to twenty years. (Such publications are listed in Chapter 11.) By contrast, it may be much harder to evaluate the performance of a private advisory account or brokerage account.

Another part of the "goldfish bowl" effect is the strict regulation of mutual funds by the U.S. Securities and Exchange Commission (SEC). Regulation does not prevent investment managers from making mistakes of judgment, but it does prevent them from taking deliberate advantage of their shareholders. In this respect, the SEC has been tough and effective. Brokers and investment advisers are regulated also, but not as effectively from the standpoint of the individual investor. All investments require careful watching, but with a good mutual fund you can sleep more soundly than with most.

Simplified Accounting

A final advantage of mutual funds is the convenience of owning a single security, as compared with owning 10 or 20 (or more) individual stocks or bonds. Your purchase and sale records are greatly simplified; you receive dividends from a single fund instead of dividends and/or interest from many sources. At income tax time, a blizzard of paperwork is reduced to a few simple entries. You can check the market value of your holding at any time by simply multiplying the number of shares you own by the daily price published in many newspapers (see Chapter 13). No wonder many large investors prefer mutual funds as a matter of convenience.

Chapter Six

Disadvantages of Mutual Funds

Although mutual funds do a lot for the investor, they can't do everything. And there are certain needs they do not meet.

Not everyone wants professional management. Some people like to be personally involved in the choice of their investments, either alone or together with an investment adviser or stockbroker. While choosing stocks and bonds is a job best left to professionals, some amateurs have proved that they can do it successfully. Some people *enjoy* selecting and managing their own stocks so much that they wouldn't think of giving it up. Others like the pleasure and reassurance of talking to a broker or adviser regularly about their investments.

Some people believe there is extra merit in having a personal account at a brokerage firm, with their own special portfolio of securities, rather than sharing in the larger portfolio of a mutual fund. We might call this "the mystique of the separate account," and as far as the funds are concerned, we don't think it's a real disadvantage. There's a supposed attraction about having a portfolio selected specifically for you and adjusted to your personal needs and objectives. But unless your needs are quite unusual, it's probable that they can be met by a selection of the types of funds we will discuss. An interesting phenomenon of recent years is that many pension funds, which traditionally maintained separate investment accounts, have noted that their results fell short of what they could have achieved through the better mutual funds, and have begun putting their money in the funds instead.

You may want a broker or adviser for a more practical reason. Even if you learn how to pick a good stock fund, a good bond fund, a good money market fund—how do you decide how to divide your money among them? How do you spot the times when the stocks and bonds are particularly attractive—or the times when prices are high and they may involve excessive risks? A broker or investment adviser is expected to deal with these problems. However, there are ways of solving the problem with mutual funds. You can buy "load" mutual funds with the advice of a broker (see Chapter 8), paying a commission for the broker's services. And in recent years there has been a development of advisory services that tell you not only which mutual funds to buy but also when to buy and when to sell (see Chapter 11).

Mutual funds are also not the answer for the person who wants to take higher risks by concentrating money in only a few securities. Perhaps you don't *want* diversification—perhaps you want to put half of your savings in the latest computer stock. That's your privilege; but remember that one reason for the popularity of mutual funds is precisely because so many amateurs have come to grief by refusing to diversify and failing to recognize the speculative risks involved in owning just a few securities.

A minor disadvantage of mutual funds is that the expenses of running them (including the fees paid to the management organizations) reduce the income paid out to you. But the expenses are not great—typically from 3/4 of 1% to 1¼% of assets, or about $1 per year for every $100 you have invested. So a bond fund owning bonds that yield 12% annually might only pay out 11% to you. But the 1% cut in your yield seems a modest price for the advantages of having your investment professionally managed, with most of the accounting done for you.

There is one other problem with mutual funds that isn't exactly a disadvantage, but that needs to be mentioned. To put it simply: Even professionals need to be watched. Some people think that because the funds are professionally managed, they can be bought and forgotten. That isn't true. Fund managements change—or sometimes a fine manager loses his or her touch. Even if you have bought what seems to be the best fund in the world, or a fund that suits you exactly, you need to review it regularly to see if it is doing what you expect of it, and if the reasons for owning it still apply.

Chapter Seven

Types of Mutual Funds

There are mutual funds to match every investment goal. As we explained in Chapter 3, funds are traditionally described as being primarily for "income" or primarily for "growth." But the real distinction is largely one of risk.

Basically, all funds fall into a few major groupings:

1. Money market funds.
2. Bond funds.
3. Tax-exempt bond funds.
4. Common stock funds.
5. Balanced funds.
6. Specialized funds.

Money Market Funds

We suggest you read the NO-NONSENSE FINANCIAL GUIDE TO MONEY MARKET FUNDS for a complete discussion of this very familiar type of mutual fund.

Money market funds share many of the characteristics of a bank. They are the simplest type of income fund, and they carry the lowest risk of all fund groups. They aim at maximizing safety, convenience and accessibility (liquidity). The dollars you put in the account remain constant without any fluctuation, while the fund adds dividends to your account based on whatever it can earn in the safest short-term investments—primarily very short-term loans to government entities, banks and major corporations.

Money market funds are for you if you are willing to forego maximum growth in order to have:

- Lowest risk.
- Safety.
- Liquidity.

Bond Funds

In a money market fund, your money is being used to make very short-term loans—loans that are repaid so soon that they are considered risk-free.

In a bond fund, your money is used to buy bonds, which means that you are making long-term loans, usually to the government (U.S. Treasury bonds) or to major corporations. Each bond carries a specific interest rate and is due to "mature," that is, to be repaid, at a specific future date. When you buy a bond coming due in a certain number of years, you are "locking in" that rate of interest for the life of the bond—which may be as long as 20 or 30 years.

This may sound like a sure thing. But as we suggested above, risks are not always what they seem, and locking in a long-term interest rate does involve a risk—even if the bond is of the absolute highest quality, such as a U.S. Treasury bond. As interest rates fluctuate, so does the market price of the bond. If interest rates rise while you own the bond, you will obviously wish that you had waited before investing, because by waiting, you could have earned a higher interest rate. Also, the change in the market will reduce the current market value of your bond. If your bond pays 10% interest, and if investors can now buy new bonds paying 12%, they obviously won't be willing to pay full price for your old bond. Of course, the opposite may happen—interest rates may drop, the current value of your bond will rise, and you will look like a person of foresight. The point is that no matter how "safe" a long-term bond may be—no matter how sure you are that you will eventually be paid off as promised—there is always the risk of price fluctuations depending on the trend of interest rates.

All of this applies equally to long-term bond *funds,* which are simply mutual funds consisting of pools of long-term bonds. At any given time, a long-term bond fund will probably give you a higher current return than a money market fund—the higher return is your reward for taking the risk of these price fluctuations. But interest rate trends are notoriously hard to predict and unless the investor badly needs the extra return, bond funds should be bought only with caution.

Bond funds are an income-oriented moderate-risk investment. They will probably give you a better return over the long run than money market funds, but be warned that they will decline in price when interest rates are rising. (See Table B at the back of this book.)

Tax-exempt Bond Funds

There is a special type of bond fund that is deservedly popular with many investors. These are the funds that invest in tax-exempt bonds—the so-called municipal bonds or "municipals" that are issued by states and municipalities and state and local agencies. The income from these bonds is *exempt from federal income tax* (unlike U.S. government bonds, which are *not* exempt from federal income tax).

The advantage of such bonds is simple. Say that you are in a 40% federal income tax bracket, and you have a choice between a U.S. Treasury bond paying 12% and a high grade tax-exempt bond paying 9%:

	Treasury Bond	*Tax-exempt Bond*
Yield before tax	12.0%	9.0%
Tax (40%)	4.8	-
Net yield after tax	7.2%	9.0%

This type of calculation—which of course varies depending on an individual's tax bracket and the specific bonds being considered—has led great numbers of investors to municipal bonds. Tax-exempt bond *funds* have relieved investors of the problems of buying and selling individual bond issues.

What about the price risks in municipal bonds? Here, too, as in the government and corporate bonds discussed above, current market prices will fluctuate depending on the level of interest rates. The difference is that, at least in recent years, the interest rates on tax-exempt bonds have been high enough to give investors substantial rewards for taking this price risk.

While the interest on municipal bonds is exempt from federal income taxes, it is usually *not* exempt from state and local taxes, except in the state where the bond is issued. In states such as New York and California where state income taxes are substantial, there are now a few funds that invest only in bonds issued in that state, and that are "double tax-exempt"—exempt from federal income taxes *and* from income taxes in the particular state where issued.

Tax-exempt bond funds are also income oriented. The investor in a higher tax bracket may realize sufficient benefit from the tax exemption to more than compensate for the moderate risk. (See Table C at the back of this book.)

Common Stock Funds

With common stock funds, we leap to the opposite end of the investment spectrum. (We suggest you read the NO-NONSENSE

FINANCIAL GUIDE TO COMMON STOCKS for additional information.) Risks are higher, and the value of your investment fluctuates quite sharply from month to month and even from day to day. There is no guarantee of your investment, and no assurance as to what growth the fund will achieve or what dividends (income) it will pay.

Why take these risks? Because common stock funds give you the opportunity for much *greater growth* than any other type of fund.

Here's why: Common stocks are shares of ownership in major corporations. Historically, as these corporations have grown and profited, the values of their stocks have gone up. At the same time, that portion of the corporation's profits not needed in the business can be paid out to shareholders (including the mutual funds that own shares) in the form of dividends.

Also, *over the long term the values of stocks have adjusted upward for inflation.* So stock prices have had a double growth component:

1. A component representing the real growth of the corporations; and
2. An adjustment to inflation.

Over the long run, investors in common stocks have done far better, on the average, than investors in banks, money market investments, or bonds. But the short-term road can be bumpy. Common stocks are traded (bought and sold) actively on the New York Stock Exchange and several other markets. The stock of a particular company tends to fluctuate in price depending on the fortunes of its industry and the relative results of the company within the industry. In addition, the price of a stock is likely to be affected by broad swings in the economy, as well as by world affairs and psychological swings in the stock market.

The funds that own common stocks share many of these characteristics. But because a fund is diversified by owning many different stock issues, the fluctuations are milder and the risks are less. A few poorly performing stocks should not upset the performance of the whole portfolio.

There are many different types of common stock funds, classified according to the degree of risk they take.

1. "Aggressive growth" or "maximum capital gain" or "maximum capital appreciation" funds take the greatest risks

in pursuit of growth. Some of them have remarkable long-term records, but their shares are likely to suffer sharp price drops when the stock market goes down. These funds may use speculative investment techniques, and they may intentionally be *less* diversified than the average fund. Obviously, if you intend to invest in funds of this type, you should take extra care, and be willing to stay with the fund long enough to ride out possible short-term market setbacks. (See Table A at the back of this book.)

2. "Growth" or "long-term growth" funds tend to be a notch lower on the risk scale and their shares may fluctuate somewhat less sharply in price than those classified as "aggressive growth." In this group, too, the best funds have very impressive long-term growth records. Generally, these funds put less emphasis on aggressive trading techniques and more emphasis on investing in companies expected to show better-than-average long-run growth trends. The quality of research is a key factor. It's worth noting that if companies grow successfully, their ability to pay dividends also increases, so some growth funds state their objective as "long-term growth of capital and income." But the current income dividends that growth funds pay are only incidental and are likely to be small. Sometimes you will see "small company growth funds" listed as a separate category; these funds concentrate on investing in fast-growing smaller companies, and they may be somewhat more volatile than the average growth fund, though the differences generally are not great. (See Table A at the back of this book.)

3. "Growth and income" funds usually put primary emphasis on growth, but they are likely to invest in larger, more stable companies that pay dividends. These funds may show less dramatic growth but also less price volatility (price swings). For the person who has not previously invested in common stock funds, one of these middle-of-the-road funds may be a natural first choice. Although you may not be interested in receiving income dividends, you should note that they add an element of stability to the fund's total performance, since the dividends are generally much more dependable year-to-year than the hoped-for growth in value of the fund's shares. The dividends are a relatively *predictable* element in the fund's total performance. (See Chapter 10.) If you don't need to spend the dividends, you simply instruct the fund to reinvest them automatically in additional shares, as many shareholders do. (See Table A at the back of this book.).

4. "Common stock income" funds carry discretion a step

further, stressing income ahead of growth and thus further reducing risk. This policy usually involves strong concentration in the stocks of larger, dividend-paying companies; it may also mean the inclusion of some bonds and/or preferred stocks for stability and extra income. (*Preferred* stocks carry the promise of a stated dividend rate if the company's profits are adequate to pay it; *common* stocks carry no certainty as to dividends.) This category of funds is often termed "equity income" funds, or "income funds—common stock policy." (See Table A at the back of this book.)

A word of caution: in common stock funds, the quality of the management can be far more important than the fund's classification. There are a few outstanding "equity income" funds that have outperformed most of the funds in the "growth" and the "aggressive growth" groups—and with far less risk. Remember also that the lines between these various groups are far from exact, funds in adjacent groups may resemble each other greatly, and the only way to be sure of a fund's classification is to study the fund's own record and policies. (See Chapter 12.)

There are also common stock funds that only invest in certain industries, such as energy, technology, or health care. And there is a small group of funds that invest only in gold mining stocks—a group that often performs spectacularly when the price of gold is rising, but poorly when the gold market turns downward.

Common stock funds are for you if you are willing to take some risks in order to achieve greater long-term growth. It's important to make up your mind about the degree of risk you feel comfortable with, and then to pick your individual fund (or funds) carefully.

Balanced Funds

The portfolio of a balanced fund includes both stocks and bonds, with the objective of reducing risk. It's a traditional form of diversification, and the policy may suit an investor who wishes to be conservative. (You can achieve much the same result and have your own "balanced" portfolio by owning both common stock funds and bond funds, picking the funds that seem best to you in each category. See Table A at the back of this book.)

Specialized Funds

The fund industry also offers mutual funds for various specialized types of portfolios. There are funds that invest in options, funds that invest primarily in foreign securities, etc. These are for the specialized investor. Based on their past records, these funds have performed no better than, and perhaps not as well as, the common stock funds in the major groups discussed above. (See Table A at the back of this book.)

Chapter Eight

How to Pick the Right Mutual Fund: Load vs. No-load

Selecting mutual funds takes a little thought and consideration. But it's no great mystery. In Chapter 7 we talked about the different types of mutual funds. How much current income do you need? What degree of risk do you wish to take to make your money grow? Do you worry when the price of your fund fluctuates? How much stability do you need to sleep well at night?

If you find it difficult to answer these questions, consider consulting with an experienced broker or salesperson. Better to pay a sales commission than have investments that do not really fit your situation. And the commission may be justified simply in terms of peace of mind.

All mutual funds can be divided into two categories: load and no-load. In some funds, you buy shares with the help and advice of a broker or salesperson, and pay a sales commission ("load"). In other funds, you do without the broker or salesperson and you pay no commission.

This is the simple difference between "load" and "no-load" funds. While the lines between the two groups are becoming slightly blurred, the typical load fund deducts a sales commission ("load") of up to 8½% of your investment. This "load" goes primarily to pay the broker or salesperson. On the other hand, the "no-load" funds stress that you buy their shares at net asset value (see Chapter 9)—your total investment goes directly into the fund, without any deduction.

A Bit of History

The easiest way to understand the differences between these two types of funds is with a touch of history. Twenty or thirty years ago, most funds were load funds. They were sold primarily by salespersons who worked for brokerage firms of various types ("broker-dealers," to use the technical term) or for the fund organizations themselves. The commissions charged on mutual fund shares were higher than those on ordinary stocks and bonds, since the customer wasn't expected to buy and sell them frequently, and the salesperson had to earn enough on the initial purchase to last for some time in the future.

But a number of no-load funds were already in existence, selling mainly by mail order to investors who were willing to do their own homework, send away for fund literature, make their own choices, and thereby save the sales commissions.

As time went on, more and more investors became aware of no-load funds and took the do-it-yourself approach. Then, in the 1970s, the boom in money market funds (almost all of which are no-load) introduced a whole new generation to the mutual fund concept and to no-load funds in particular. When these money market fund investors began to buy other mutual funds, such as bond funds and common stock funds, they expected the same no-load arrangement they were used to—and more and more fund organizations gave it to them.

So now, if you are willing to do your own homework, the range of no-load funds available to you is virtually as great as the choice of load funds.

Are No-load Funds Worth the Trouble?

Is it worth doing your homework and research in order to select no-load funds intelligently? Actually, if you have the inclination, tracking the funds and selecting the ones that are right for you can be *fun*. And it does make a difference. See what happens, in the following table, to two investments of $1,000 each in two funds that both achieve an identical 12% average growth rate. But while one fund is no-load, the other charges an 8.5% load—so that $85 of the $1,000 goes to the sales organization, and only $915 is actually invested for you:

	No-load	*Load*	*Difference*
Initial Investment	$ 1,000	$ 1,000	$ 0
Initial Value	1,000	915	85
Value of Investment after:*			
1 year	1,120	1,025	95
5 years	1,762	1,613	149
10 years	3,106	2,842	264
20 years	9,646	8,826	820
30 years	29,960	27,413	2,547

*Assuming reinvestment of all distributions and total growth rate of 12% annually.

Does the load always take so deep a bite? Not always. Some funds charge a load of less than 8.5%. The charge is almost always lower in percentage terms when you invest a large amount—say above $10,000—and you can receive this reduced rate if you make smaller purchases during the year that total the required amount.

On the other hand, you should be aware that the commission is really higher in percentage terms than the industry says. The example in the table above shows what the load funds call an 8.5% load. But since the net price of the shares without commission is actually $915, the commission would be calculated in most sales situations as $85/915, or 9.3%.

So there is reason to learn how to pick no-load funds for yourself. In Chapter 10 we will begin to discuss how to go about it.

How Do No-load Funds Make Money?

If the no-loads don't charge a commission, how do they make their money? The answer is that the managers of all funds—load and no-load—charge the fund an advisory fee to cover their management expenses. This fee is one of the regular annual expenses of the fund, and has nothing to do with the sales commission. The sales commission (load), if there is one, goes to pay the salesperson or broker and the sales organization. The no-loads don't have salespersons or elaborate sales organizations, and generally finance their selling effort out of the advisory fee.

Which Is Better—Load or No-load?

Are load funds better than no-loads? The load fund industry used to claim that they were—arguing, in effect, that you can't get something for nothing. But it's been well demonstrated that sales charges have nothing to do with management skills and investment performance. The two groups of funds have, on the average, performed about the same. There are load funds with records ranging from excellent to poor, and there are no-loads with records ranging from excellent to poor.

Why Buy a Load Fund?

Investors' needs may differ—just as some consumers buy gasoline at self-service pumps, while others are willing to pay extra for the same gasoline in order to get full service. The important thing is to understand what you are paying for and getting. If you don't have the aptitude or inclination to select mutual funds yourself—or perhaps you simply don't have the time—a salesperson or broker who is knowledgeable and conscientious may more than earn his/her commission.

Moral

Earlier in this chapter we compared load and no-load funds with equal performance. But let's say that a salesperson or broker helps you pick a good fund with an 8.5% load that, over the years, achieves a performance rate that averages 3% better annually than the no-load fund you might have picked for yourself. In this case the load fund will make up the difference in value in a little more than three years, and over longer periods it will build up an impressive lead. Moral: Over longer periods an outstanding fund will out-perform a mediocre fund, irrespective of load.

Chapter Nine

Net Asset Value

At this point you need to know how the price of a mutual fund share is calculated.

Basically, every afternoon the mutual fund adds up the market values of the securities (stocks, bonds, etc.) it owns. (For example, if the fund owns 10,000 shares of common stock of General Motors, and General Motors finished trading or "closed" at a price of \$65 per share, the calculation is simply 10,000 × \$65 = \$650,000. And so on.) The fund also adds in the value of its other assets—its cash and any amounts it is owed. From the total it subtracts any liabilities—amounts that it owes to others for various fees and other expenses, etc. The result is the "total net assets" of the fund. This figure is then divided by the "shares outstanding" (the total number of shares held by shareholders) to arrive at the "net asset value per share," which is each share's proportionate interest in the fund's total net assets.

Obviously, if the market value of the securities the fund owns goes up, the net asset value per share will go up. And vice-versa.

On any given day, the investors who wish to put money in the fund do it by buying new shares from the fund at the net asset value calculated at the end of that day—sometimes less a commission, sometimes not (see Chapter 8). The investors who take money out of the fund do it by "redeeming" shares—selling them back to the fund—also at the day's net asset value. (Note: A few funds impose a charge on redemptions. See Chapter 18.)

Incidentally, this means that you never know at exactly what price your order for purchase or redemption will be executed. All orders received by the fund on a given day before the close of trading are executed at whatever price is calculated that day, which can only be done after the close.

The exception is the money market type of mutual fund. The money market funds make a practice of holding their share values constant—usually at \$1.00 per share—and they own securities that ordinarily show only fractional variations in market value.

The mutual fund pricing structure is honest and straightforward and works well for the shareholder. What you see is what you get.

Chapter Ten

Evaluating Performance

Before you can choose a mutual fund intelligently, you need to know how the performance of different funds is compared.

There are three ways a mutual fund can make money for its shareholders:

1. Payment of dividends.
2. Payment of capital gains distributions.
3. Increase in net asset value.

Payment of Dividends

During the year the fund receives dividends on the stocks it owns and interest on the bonds and other fixed-income securities it owns. After deducting expenses, including the management fee, what is left is "net investment income." Once a year, or in installments, the fund pays this net investment income to shareholders as "income dividends," in proportion to the number of shares owned.

Payment of Capital Gains Distributions

The fund may also "realize" capital gains—i.e. make profits for its shareholders—by selling securities for *more than* the fund paid for them. At the end of the year, if these capital *gains* outweigh any capital *losses* (i.e. from the sale of securities at *less than* the fund paid for them), the difference or "net gain" is ordinarily paid out to the shareholders as a capital gains distribution. By law, such a distribution can only be made once a year.

Increase in Net Asset Value

If the securities in the fund's portfolio rise in price, on the average, then the net asset value of the fund's shares also will rise (see Chapter 9), and the shareholder's investment will be worth more than it was before.

Calculating Performance

Years ago, fund "performance" was usually calculated by adding only capital gains distributions and any rise in net asset value. The dividends paid were shown separately as "yield." This perhaps made sense for a shareholder who wanted or needed to spend the dividend income and wanted it clearly defined, but it was often difficult to compare different fund performances fairly with each other.

Now most performance statistics are on what is called a "total return" basis, which takes all three elements into account, and shows how the value of a holder's investment would grow if all income dividends and capital gains distributions were reinvested in additional shares.

An example: Let's say that a fund starts a year with net asset value at $10.00 per share and ends with net asset value at $11.00. During the year it pays out $.40 per share in income dividends and $.70 per share in capital gains. Leaving aside certain minor adjustments, the quoted figures would be:

Yield (Dividend Income):

$$\frac{\$\,0.40}{\$10.00} = 4.0\%$$

Performance—Old Definition:

$$\frac{(\$11.00 - \$10.00) + \$0.70}{\$10.00} = +17.0\%$$

Performance—Total Return (New Definition):

$$\frac{(\$11.00 - \$10.00) + \$0.70 + \$0.40}{\$10.00} = +21.0\%$$

In a bad year, of course, the net asset value of the fund could drop, and performance could be negative rather than positive.

Performance of a fund over short or long periods may be compared with other funds or with the "market averages." For example, a growth fund may be compared with an average of many growth funds. Common stock funds are often compared with two or three well-known stock market averages that are found daily in your newspaper's financial section. One of the most popular stock market averages is the Standard & Poor's 500 Stock Index, an index made up of 500 leading stocks. The Dow-Jones Industrial Average is probably the most famous of all averages; however, as it is based on only 30 very prominent stocks, it is less of a reflection of the total market picture than the S&P "500." The New York Stock Exchange Composite Index includes all 1300-or-so stocks listed on the New York Stock Exchange and tends to move proportionately to the S&P "500."

As a typical example of how funds use these performance comparisons, here is a table published in the annual report of the Weingarten Equity Fund for June 30, 1983:

Period ended June 30, 1983	Weingarten Equity Fund Net Asset Value Per Share	Dow Jones Industrials	Standard & Poor's 500
	% Change*	% Change*	% Change*
6 months	+ 47%	+ 20%	+ 22%
12 months	+ 114%	+ 59%	+ 61%
5 years	+ 336%	+ 101%	+ 129%
10 years	+ 577%	+ 135%	+ 161%

*The Fund results assume the reinvestment of all capital gain and ordinary distribution income as of their record dates. The performance of the Fund is compared with that of the Dow Jones Industrial Average and the Standard & Poor's 500 Index, which are unmanaged and widely regarded as representative measurements of the stock market as a whole. Changes in the two indices assume reinvestment of all dividends based on data supplied by Lipper Analytical Services. The performance of the Fund should be considered in the light of its investment policy and objectives, the characteristics of the portfolio securities and the periods selected.

Chapter Eleven

Sources of Information

Even if you intend to buy funds through a broker or salesperson, it is a good idea to familiarize yourself with some of the reliable sources of mutual fund information. If you are ready to do your own homework, you may find the prospect interesting and even exciting. And some of the sources that report on mutual fund performance and other statistics will also help you out with recommendations. They can't advise you as to what type of fund is right for you, but within the different groups they will help you in selecting better-quality funds.

Some publications show mutual fund performance for periods as short as the latest month or latest three months. This may be interesting, but you need a publication that shows how funds have done over longer periods—at least five years, preferably ten. You also need a source that classifies funds by type—that is, by investment objective—which is true of most of the sources listed below.

We have listed a few of the better publications, dividing them into those that provide performance statistics only and those that provide statistics plus recommendations. Some of these publications are too expensive to be practical for the average individual, but may be carried by your local library—ask your librarian what's available. Or you may be able to consult them at a mutual fund office or investment firm.

Performance Statistics Only

Lipper Mutual Fund Performance Analysis (Lipper Analytical Distributors, 74 Trinity Place, New York, N.Y. 10006): This is the industry's leading source of performance statistics, and is widely quoted in other publications. Very expensive, and subscribed to primarily by professionals, but you may be able to find it at a library or elsewhere (see above). Issued weekly; special quarterly issues show performance over longer periods (usually five and ten years).

Computer Directions Advisors: Another detailed service primarily for professionals.

Performance Statistics and Other Data

Wiesenberger Investment Companies Service (Wiesenberger Financial Services, 1633 Broadway, New York, N.Y. 10019): The Wiesenberger annual yearbook is the bible of the fund industry, with extensive descriptions of funds, many chapters of information about the industry, all sorts of other data, and plentiful performance statistics. It is found in many libraries. There are also quarterly performance supplements.

Barron's: This national financial weekly (generally available on newsstands and at libraries) publishes special mutual fund surveys quarterly (in mid-February, May, August and November) featuring articles and some performance statistics.

Statistics and Recommendations

United Mutual Fund Selector (210 Newbury Street, Boston, MA 02116): Annual subscription $98. This excellent semimonthly newsletter features articles, performance statistics, and a recommended "Supervised List" of about 30 common stock funds classified by objective.

The No-Load Fund Investor (P.O. Box 283, Hastings-on-Hudson, N.Y. 10706): *The Annual Handbook for No-Load Fund Investors* is $29; the *Handbook* plus four quarterly supplements is $46. Not quite as complete as Wiesenberger, but exceptionally useful and an excellent value. The quarterly statistics classify funds by objective, are clear and easy to read, and include recommendations.

Growth Fund Guide (Box 6600, Rapid City, SD 57709): Annual subscription $79. An excellent monthly publication covering selected no-load funds. Emphasizes the more aggressive growth funds, but lists a few middle-of-the-road funds as well. Recommendations classified by objective.

Forbes Magazine (generally available): Every year in August, *Forbes* publishes a mutual fund survey featuring ten-year performance records of all funds, a few other statistics, and a brief "honor roll" of outstanding funds. Instead of the usual classifications, *Forbes* gives its own rankings of how funds have performed relatively in "up" and "down" markets.

In Sum

The recommendations of these sources are reasonably intelligent and fair, but don't hesitate to apply your own judgment to what you read. Look for funds that appear to fit your own particular objectives and preferences. Remember that even the best past record doesn't guarantee what a fund will achieve in the future.

Above all, don't pick a fund simply because it is near the top of the performance ratings for the latest year. A fund can do well over short periods for the wrong reasons—sometimes because management took more risks than really are prudent. But if a fund has done exceptionally well over a ten-year period, and still seems to be doing well, management apparently knows what it is doing.

Understanding the Statistics

A few warnings regarding performance statistics are in order:

1. Most of the statistics are presented in terms of percentage increases (+) or decreases (−). Sometimes the decreases may be shown by parentheses (25%) instead of a minus sign. Make sure you know how to read these. Here is how a $10,000 investment would end up with various percentage changes:

−75% or (75%)	$ 2,500
−50% or (50%)	5,000
−25% or (25%)	7,500
0%	10,000
+25%	12,500
+50%	15,000
+100%	20,000
+150%	25,000
+200%	30,000
+300%	40,000
+400%	50,000

2. Remember that if the percentage figures are on a "total return" basis, any dividend yield is included. The statistics may also show yield separately, as a matter of interest; but don't add this in to the total again.

3. If the statistics compare fund performance with stock market averages such as the Dow Jones Industrial Average or the Standard & Poor's 500 Stock Index, be careful. Fund performance will probably include income dividends ("yield"); but the market averages do *not* include income dividends, unless the publication makes a special adjustment. It's not hard for a fund to outshine the market averages if the fund is credited with 4% or 6% annually in income dividends and the averages are not. Read the footnotes carefully.

Contacting the Funds

When you have picked a few funds that look suitable, the next step is to send for their literature. Some of the publications named above do not include fund addresses or phone numbers. But you can get lists of funds by type, including addresses, from the Investment Company Institute, 1775 K Street, N.W., Washington, D.C. 20006 (202-293-7700), the trade association of the mutual fund industry. Ask them also for their general information booklets on funds. Lists covering no-load funds only are available from the No-Load Mutual Fund Association, Inc., 11 Penn Plaza, Suite 2204, New York, N.Y. 10001 (212-563-4540). You'll note that most of the major funds have toll-free "800" phone numbers that make it simple to request their literature.

Chapter Twelve

How to Read a Prospectus and Financial Report

When you request information, a fund will typically send you a prospectus (a legal document that is the basic description of the fund and its policies) and its latest annual and quarterly reports to shareholders, as well as some miscellaneous sales literature.

Reading the Shareholder Reports

Most funds send reports to shareholders on a quarterly basis. These usually include a letter that reports on the fund's performance and current investment policies, and a list of the fund's investments ("portfolio"). The annual and semiannual reports include full financial statements showing the income and performance of the fund. (The financial statements may or may not be repeated in the prospectus.)

Read the letter to shareholders. What do the portfolio managers have to say about the current economic situation? How do they plan to act in the future? Does their investment outlook make sense to you? Are their goals the same as yours? Do they give a clear picture of what the fund has done over the last three, six or twelve months?

Look at the portfolio list. See what types of securities the fund owns. Are you comfortable with them? Are the holdings varied in a way that makes sense to you? The fund may list its holdings by specific industry, or it may use such broad headings as "cyclical stocks," "consumer industries," etc.

Reading the Prospectus

Prospectuses are something of a puzzle. A fund can't legally sell shares to you until you have first received its prospectus. Over the years, mutual fund prospectuses have become weighted down with large quantities of legal verbiage that don't really help you understand the fund and its policies. But now there has been a change. Beginning in late 1984, the SEC has not only permitted but actually ordered the funds to provide a shorter, simplified prospectus, with additional information available from the fund on request. This should help. Read the short form, and phone the fund office for the "Statement of Additional Information" if you still have questions that haven't been answered.

Nothing in the prospectus is more important than the statement of the fund's investment objective and policies. Read it carefully. Some of it may sound excessively legal, but the industry trend is toward greater clarity and simplicity. Despite the occasional fuzziness and ritualistic language, you should be able to get some idea of whether the fund's policies match what you are looking for, and whether you can feel comfortable with its approach.

Diversified and Non-diversified

You will notice that most funds are described in their prospectus as "diversified." A few are listed as "non-diversified." These are legal definitions. They sound important but in reality the difference is not great.

A "diversified" fund must keep *75%* of its total portfolio diversified so that no single investment in that segment can make up more than 5% of the fund's total assets. (In the remaining 25% of the portfolio, management is free to concentrate in one or more larger positions if so desired.) A "non-diversified" company is only required to diversify *50%* of its total portfolio and can concentrate investments within the remaining 50%.

Management

The prospectus will tell you about the management firm and its affiliations, and who the directors and officers are. Most funds are required to have a certain number of directors who are *not* affiliated with the management firm; the law gives these "independent directors" many responsibilities intended to ensure fair treatment of the fund by the manager.

Management Fees

The fee paid to the fund's manager—termed the "investment advisory fee," or "management fee"—is generally the fund's largest single expense. The way the fee is calculated is stated in the prospectus. Most fees are calculated as a percentage of assets, and the fees usually work out to between 0.4% and 1.0% annually of the net assets.

If a fund's performance is well above average, don't be afraid of a higher-than-average fee; it's simply the manager's reward for having done a good job.

Fund Expenses

Let us turn back for a moment to the financial statements in the fund's shareholder reports. Near the bottom of the "Statement of Per Share Capital and Income Changes" you will find a figure representing the fund's "expense ratio." The expense ratio is the percentage relationship between a year's expenses and the fund's total net assets. It generally ranges from 0.5% to 1.5%—occasionally higher. If a fund receives dividends and interest on its portfolio that amount to 8.0% of average assets for a given year, and if the expense ratio for the year is 1.0%, then there will be 7.0% left to distribute to shareholders as income dividends.

How important is the expense ratio? If you buy a fund strictly for dividend yield, a high expense ratio is a disadvantage. But in a good growth fund, the expense ratio is a minor factor relative to total performance. If a fund has achieved a good past record in the face of a high expense ratio, there is no reason why it shouldn't continue to do so in the future. A high expense ratio doesn't usually mean poor management; more often it reflects a fund that is small in size, or a management fee that is a higher percentage than average.

Other Information

The prospectus will give you all sorts of additional information. It will tell you about the various shareholder conveniences described in Chapter 5. (Make sure the fund has the ones you want.) It will tell you when the fund pays dividends. It will tell you when the fund's fiscal (accounting) year ends, and when reports to shareholders are issued. (Annual reports must be mailed within 60 days after the close of the fiscal year; new prospectuses must be ready within 120 days.) It will tell you what organization (sometimes a bank, sometimes not) acts as the fund's shareholder servicing agent or transfer agent, and what bank (in this case it *must* be a bank) acts as custodian of the fund's cash and securities.

In either the annual report or the prospectus, or sometimes in both, you will find a certain amount of data on performance. By law there must be a ten-year table of "per share capital and income changes," showing for each year the change in the fund's net asset value per share and the income dividends and capital gains distributions paid. You can calculate "total return" performance from these figures, but the table is not really convenient to use. Somewhere in the literature most funds include a more useful item, a chart showing an "illustration of an assumed investment of $10,000"—a chart showing how $10,000 invested in the fund would have grown over the last 10, 15 or 20 years, or for the whole life of the fund. The chart is usually clear enough, but the time period covered may be one that makes the figures hard to compare with those published by other funds. For comparisons of performance, you'll probably find that the figures compiled in the reference sources mentioned in Chapter 11 are easier and more practical to use than those published by the funds themselves.

Now we'll look at those sections of the prospectus that tell you how to go about purchasing and redeeming shares.

Ordering Shares

In a *load* fund, the prospectus will tell you exactly how the load is calculated, and your broker or salesperson will explain the purchasing procedures. Most *no-load* funds enclose an order form with their prospectus and ask you to return the order form with a check. A smaller number will take your order by phone and send you a bill. (You must pay within five business days.) Some funds that require a written application to start will then take subsequent orders by phone once the account is opened.

There are a few details about ordering shares that may not be made clear on the order form. If you are opening a joint account, note that joint accounts in the securities industry do *not* operate on the same "either/or" basis as the usual joint account with a bank, where either owner acting alone can deposit or withdraw freely. Instead, the signatures of *both* owners are required on all important matters, including the redemption of shares. If you are purchasing shares for a minor, the usual procedure is to use the custodian arrangement permitted under the Uniform Gifts to Minors Acts in effect in all states. The correct form of registration is "Nancy Jones (one adult only) as custodian for David Jones (one minor only) under the Uniform Gifts to Minors Act of (state of residence of the minor)." The Social Security number given for the account should be that of the minor.

One piece of information that you will *not* find in the prospectus is a list of the states in which the fund's shares are registered for sale. If a fund is not registered for sale in the state in which you are a resident, you cannot buy shares in that fund. Even though the funds go through a careful registration process with the SEC every year, most of the states require separate registrations before the fund can be sold in that particular state. Most of the major funds are available for sale in all 50 states and the District of Columbia, but the cost and trouble of state registrations discourages some smaller funds from registering widely. For a load fund, your broker should know where the fund is registered; in the case of a no-load fund, phone the fund office or consult the Wiesenberger handbook.

Minimums

The prospectus will clearly state minimum purchase requirements. A typical fund may require $250 or $500 to open an account and a minimum of $100 on subsequent purchases. But the minimums vary widely. Some funds reserve the right to redeem accounts that fall below the initial minimum, in order to save the fund the expense of maintaining a large number of small accounts.

Fractional Shares

Almost all mutual funds have accounting systems that can credit shareholders with fractional shares to three decimal places. For example, if you send a check for $1,000 to a no-load fund, and the fund is priced at $18.50 per share on the day your order is received, you will be credited with 54.054 shares. The fractional shares make it simple to buy or redeem shares in any desired dollar amount, with no odd pennies or dollars left over. If you insist on receiving stock certificates for your shares, you will find that the shareholder servicing agent won't issue certificates for fractional shares, and the fractions will have to be left on deposit. Most mutual fund shareholders have learned that it's far easier to leave all shares on deposit, and that stock certificates are an antiquated nuisance—particularly when you want to redeem the shares and the certificates have to be submitted (see Chapter 18).

Redemption Procedures

When you read a fund's prospectus, make sure that you understand the redemption procedures (see Chapter 18). And after you become a fund shareholder, when the fund mails you a new prospectus annually (as most funds do), see if the redemption section lists any new procedures. At some point you will probably want to redeem (sell) at least part of your shares, and when that time comes you don't want any surprises.

Chapter Thirteen

How to Read the Newspaper Quotations

One major advantage of a mutual fund is the ease with which you can follow the performance of a fund and the daily value of your investment. Every day, mutual fund prices are listed in the financial section of many newspapers, including the nationally available *Wall Street Journal.* Your fund may be listed in its alphabetical place, or, if it is part of a major fund group, under the group heading (Dreyfus, Fidelity, Oppenheimer, Vanguard, etc.). Here is an excerpt from the *Wall Street Journal* listing showing prices of May 31, 1984:

	NAV	Offer Price	NAV Chg.
Shrm Dean	6.86	N.L.	+.08
Sierra Gro	10.61	N.L.	+.06
Sigma Funds:			
Capitl Sh	11.21	12.25	+.03
Incm Shr	6.74	7.37	+.03
Invest Sh	6.78	7.41	+.02
Special	6.23	6.81	+.03
Trust Sh	9.91	10.83	...
Venture	8.34	9.11	+.03
Sm Barney	12.32	N.L.	+.06
Sm BrIncG	8.01	8.50	...
So GenFnd	13.10	13.72	−.02

The fund names, obviously, are drastically abbreviated, but you will learn to recognize the funds you are interested in. The example shows a fund group (the Sigma funds) and several individual funds that are not part of a large group.

"NAV" is the net asset value per share for each fund, calculated at the close of business on the given date (see Chapter 9). It is also the price that the fund paid for shares redeemed on that day (except in the infrequent cases where a redemption fee is charged). The "Offer Price" (offering price) column shows the price paid by investors who bought shares on that day—the net asset value plus the commission or "load." The abbreviation "N.L." means that the fund is *no-load* and that the price was the same for purchases as for redemptions—net asset value, with no commission added.

The right-hand column shows the change in net asset value compared with the previous day. Stock market prices averaged slightly higher on May 31, 1984 than the previous day, so most of the funds showed modest gains in net asset value. However,

SoGen International Fund was down in value by $.02 per share. Sigma Trust Shares and Smith, Barney Income and Growth Fund each showed no change on the day.

Some listings may show "bid" and "asked" instead of "NAV" and "Offering Price." These are old trading terms; the logic is that the fund will "bid" a certain price to buy your shares from you when you redeem, and will "ask" a certain price (the same price, in the case of a no-load fund) when you want to purchase shares from it.

When a fund price drops sharply because the shares have gone "ex-dividend" (see Chapter 16) that day, and the price has been marked down by the amount of the dividend, the price should be footnoted to explain this—the price in the "NAV" column might look like "x 7.66." But often the footnote is omitted. If you notice a sharp unexplained drop in the price of your fund, don't hesitate to phone the fund and ask about it. It may help to consult the prospectus to find out when dividends are usually paid.

Chapter Fourteen

One Fund or Many?

We have frequently talked about "choosing the right fund for you." Perhaps we have made it sound as though one particular fund could be expected to meet all your investment needs. Of course this isn't so.

If you have only $500 or $1,000 to invest, then on a practical basis you are better off beginning with one fund that meets your primary needs. But as your investment money grows, you can take into consideration more than one objective. You may want to have some money in a money market fund, to meet current needs and perhaps to take advantage of higher-than-normal interest rates. You may buy shares in a common stock fund for the primary objective of long-term growth. And if you are in a high tax bracket, you may also put some money in a municipal bond fund to generate tax-free income.

In addition to meeting your different objectives, this approach reduces risk by giving you even more diversification than you would have with a single fund. During a downward turn in the stock market, when your common stock fund is doing poorly, you may get particularly high income from your money fund and tax-exempt bond fund. Or the situation may be reversed. If you want the long-term growth that can come from common stocks, but find yourself worrying excessively over stock market price fluctuations, you may be particularly relieved to know that a certain percentage of your money is working in different directions.

But even if you are completely comfortable with all your money invested in common stocks, you find the price fluctuations manageable, and you don't want to sacrifice any of your growth potential, it may make sense to spread your money over a few funds rather than one. Different types of stocks perform differently at various times, and predictions are often difficult. One way to protect yourself is to divide your money among a few common stock funds with varying orientations. At the simplest level, you might own one aggressive growth fund and one growth-income fund. You can easily expand the selection as you go along to include funds that you find desirable. If you own a fund that concentrates on smaller growth companies, you may wish to add one that focuses on larger growth companies. And so on.

You might also want to put smaller slices of your money into more specialized funds. If you are worried about inflation, you might want some of your money in a gold fund, and some in a fund specializing in energy stocks. The possibilities are endless.

Even when choosing among funds of exactly the same type, diversification is usually the best policy. Which aggressive growth fund is the very best choice for the next ten years? While it's easy to see which fund in any group was the best choice for the *last* ten years, there's no way to be certain of the future. Rather than trying to decide which particular fund has the best prospects, it may be more reasonable to acknowledge the uncertainties of the situation and make up a package of a few funds that look promising. If one turns out disappointing, perhaps the others will more than make up for it.

Chapter Fifteen

When Do I Begin?

Should you try to adjust your mutual fund purchases to take advantage of market fluctuations?

Common stock prices tend to move in broad cycles. Sometimes the cycles seem to average about four years in length, but you can't be sure how any particular cycle will behave. Obviously, if you could pick one point at which to invest in common stock funds, it would be better in theory to invest at a point in the cycle when prices are low rather than when prices are high.

Bond prices also fluctuate. During most of the period since 1950, interest rates have basically been rising and, as a reflection of this, bond prices have been falling. No one really knows when this trend will end, or whether it may have already ended.

Unfortunately, predicting market movements is difficult even for the most expert professional, and an amateur can hardly hope to do better. However, an advantage of a mutual fund is that, in a diversified portfolio, movements in some portfolio securities are likely to offset movements in others, and fluctuations in the value of the fund's shares are likely to be less extreme than fluctuations in the prices of individual securities. Also, a good manager may be successful in insulating a fund to some extent from declines in the general market. But even the best-managed fund is likely to move to some extent with the general market trend.

Many amateur investors react to market fluctuations in exactly the wrong way. They tend to buy securities toward the end of a long market rise, when everyone has gotten overenthusiastic; and they panic and sell near the end of a decline, just when the market is about to turn up. There are a few useful things you can do to guard against making this kind of mistake:

1. Recognize that this is an uncertain area, and distrust the person who tells you that the market is "bound to go up" or "bound to go down."

2. Recognize that markets are subject to fads, and that fads are dangerous. Try to avoid crowd psychology. When stock prices are rising and the XYZ fund has gone up 50% and everyone tells you that this is the time to buy, be careful: prices may be near a peak.

3. Consider spacing out your purchases on a regular schedule. For the average investor, this is probably the best approach of all. If you can invest, say, $500 every three months, and keep this up over a period of years, you will do some buying when prices are high and some when prices are low, and you will end up with a reasonable cost average over the long term without running the danger of having to make market predictions. This approach is often termed "dollar-cost averaging." For example, if you have never bought a mutual fund and if, at the end of reading this book, you have decided to take $10,000 out of a savings account to buy a good common stock fund—don't do your buying all at once. Space it out in installments over a year or two. In that way, if it happens to be a period when prices are declining, you won't have the depressing experience of having completed all your buying just before the market dips.

This kind of regular purchase program does more than simply guarantee you a reasonable average cost. If you develop the habit of making regular purchases and stick to it over the years, you will have achieved the kind of long-run savings program that almost everyone intends to follow but that few people actually achieve. As you build up a savings cushion, you are likely to find that market fluctuations become less and less a source of worry, and that your money is managing to compound and grow beyond your expectations.

Chapter Sixteen

Timing and Dividends

Although we have already discussed dividends (Chapter 10), we haven't mentioned a small point about the relation of dividends to the timing of your mutual fund purchases.

When a fund's board of directors declares a dividend and sets a payment date, it also sets the "ex-dividend" date ("ex-dividend" means "without dividend"). New shares purchased on this date (or after) are no longer entitled to receive the dividend. But this really doesn't matter, since, as an offset, the *price per share* is *automatically marked down exactly by the amount of the dividend.*

So don't ever let anyone tell you to buy shares of a mutual fund before a certain date, in order to "get the dividend." You get the dividend, sure enough, but you pay a higher price because of it.

It makes more sense to buy *after* the ex-dividend date. Here's why: Putting aside market variations, the price you pay on the ex-dividend date or later, as we said above, is marked down precisely to compensate you for not getting the dividend. *But since you don't receive the dividend, you don't have to pay income tax on it.* If you buy before the ex-date, the dividend you get offsets the higher price you pay, but you are actually worse off by the amount of the tax you will have to pay on the dividend.

So when a fund is about to pay a dividend or capital gains distribution—especially a big one—wait to buy until after the ex-dividend date.

As pointed out in Chapter 13, the newspaper listings often fail to show the "ex-dividend" price changes correctly. When a fund's price drops sharply because the shares have gone "ex-dividend" that day, there should be a footnote of explanation. But often the footnote is omitted. (See Chapter 13 for more on this point.)

Chapter Seventeen

To Sell or Not to Sell

Deciding when to sell mutual fund shares can be just as puzzling as deciding when to buy. Again, an amateur should be wary of believing anyone who claims to know just what the stock market or bond market is about to do. But again, there are some guidelines that will help you make your selling decisions intelligently.

There are three basic situations in which you are likely to consider selling (redeeming) fund shares:

Reason for Redeeming #1—To Raise Cash

You need money—perhaps unexpectedly, perhaps as part of a long-range plan. If it is a planned event—if you are buying a house, or taking out money for a child's college tuition—don't wait until the last minute, since you might be forced to redeem just at a time when the market is depressed. Consider redeeming 6 to 18 months before you actually need the money, and let the cash sit safely in a money market fund or bank market rate account until you are ready to use it.

Reason for Redeeming #2—To Switch

What if you have doubts about a particular fund you own? An investment in a good fund doesn't have to be watched as closely as an individual stock, but neither can you ignore it entirely. Every few months (or as frequently as you wish) you should review your holdings carefully and ask yourself the following questions:

- Has there been any change in my investment situation or objective?
- Am I satisfied with the fund(s) I own?
- If I were starting fresh today, would I pick the same fund(s) that I actually now own?

The last question is critical. If there are reasons to prefer a fund you don't own over one you do, think carefully. If the reasons are serious and not trivial, don't hesitate to switch. Even the best fund sometimes turns mediocre. Sometimes a good manager simply doesn't cope well with a new and different stage in the economy. No matter how well a fund has served you, *don't become emotionally attached to it.* On the other hand, don't switch out of a good fund just because it has shown poor performance for a very short period.

If your fund shares are now worth more than they originally cost you, you may have a capital gains tax to pay if you sell (see Chapter 20). But it is probably a mistake to let this stand in your way. Paying the tax is usually a modest price to pay for following your best judgment and being invested in the funds that appear to suit you best right now. If you have held the fund shares long enough to qualify for long-term capital gains treatment, any tax will be quite modest. (Note that a new tax law, passed in 1984, will shorten this required holding period to only six months and one day, from the previous one year and one day.)

Reason for Redeeming #3—Market Conditions

Some investors like to sell their mutual fund shares when they feel that the stock market (or the bond market, as the case may be) is in danger of a major decline, in the hope of avoiding the decline and perhaps buying back their shares at a lower price.

Logically at least, this makes sense. The stock market does move in cycles, and if you can sell at the top and buy at the bottom you will certainly be well off. The trouble is that the timing of these cycles is quite uncertain, and while the major turning points are easy to see in retrospect a year or two later, they can be very hard to recognize when they are taking place. Many investors, unfortunately, sell their shares in the panic atmosphere that exists when the stock market is near a low point, which is just the time when it would be best to buy. They then either (1) fail to buy the shares back or (2) buy them at just the wrong time—when everyone has become enthusiastic and stock prices are at or near a high point.

So the average investor is probably better off simply buying and holding mutual fund shares for the long pull—and spacing out fund purchases as discussed in Chapter 15 so that all buying is not concentrated near a market top.

However, if you decide that you do want to try to "catch" these cycles, here are a few thoughts to keep in mind.

Stock Market Fluctuations

While stock market cycles are usually hard to judge at the time they are taking place, there are some indicators that professional investors use to try to understand and forecast price movements.

Some of these indicators depend on the state of the economy; some are based on the patterns of the stock market itself. The stock market often anticipates changes in the economy. Major market upturns have often begun near the end of a recession, when everyone is full of doom and gloom. Major downturns have often begun near the end of a period of prosperity and rising interest rates. If you want to "catch the cycle" successfully, you need to have the courage to buy when most people are gloomy and sell when most people are enthusiastic.

Long-term Headaches in the Bond Market

In Chapter 7, we explained why we think that the average investor may be better off avoiding long-term bonds and long-term bond funds. Movements in interest rates and bond prices have been even more difficult to predict than movements in the stock market. But while the long-term trend in stock prices has been *upward*—rewarding the common stock investor who rode out the fluctuations—the long-term trend in bond prices for most of the postwar period has been *downward*—reflecting the long, grinding climb in interest rates. So rather than advising you when to sell long-term bonds, we will repeat our earlier advice: invest in them only with great caution.

Tax-exempts: Whether to Buy and Hold

In Chapter 7 we also explained that for someone in a high tax bracket, the high net yield after taxes available from a tax-exempt fund might justify taking the risk of a price decline. If you think you can predict when such a decline in bond prices is coming, of course it makes sense to sell. But if tax-exempt income is what you need, it's equally reasonable simply to pick a fund that has had an outstanding record over several years, hope that the yield will be high enough to compensate for any price declines, and hope that the fund managers will be smart enough to hold such declines to a minimum.

Chapter Eighteen

How to Redeem Your Shares

Having discussed the reasons why you might wish to sell your mutual fund shares, we would like to discuss briefly the procedures you will need to follow when you decide to redeem.

Remember that mutual fund shares are not traded on an open market like most common stocks. Rather, the fund itself stands ready to redeem (buy back) your shares on any business day when you wish to sell. The redemption price is the net asset value per share (see Chapter 9) calculated on the day the fund receives your order. However, your order will only be valid if you follow the fund's stated procedures.

Read this part of your fund's prospectus carefully. Most funds—or their shareholder servicing agents—require a letter of instructions with signature(s) guaranteed, for a redemption. If there are joint owners, all owners must sign the letter, and all signatures must be guaranteed. A guarantee protects against an unauthorized person redeeming your shares. You must secure this guarantee from your commercial bank or from a brokerage firm that is a member of a national securities exchange. Note that most funds do *not* accept guarantees by savings banks or savings and loan associations. If you hold certificates for shares being redeemed, the certificates must also be submitted, with guaranteed signatures on the reverse or on an accompanying "stock power" form. (This, again, is a reason to leave your shares on deposit with the agent and not to bother holding certificates.)

Some funds waive the signature guarantee requirement on smaller redemptions, especially if the stock is in the name of a single owner. When there are joint owners, the fund usually wants to be sure that one owner is not redeeming without the knowledge of the other. In the case of trusts, estates, corporations or other entities, the fund will often require additional documents for redemption—check with the fund or servicing agent in advance.

Under the law, the fund must mail a check to you within seven days after the redemption date. However, this mailing may be delayed if you bought your shares just before redeeming them and your purchase check hasn't yet cleared.

Redemptions by telephone are common in money market funds, but are not usually permitted by other types of funds. However, if your fund is part of a "family of funds," you can probably arrange for *switches* by telephone. If the group has a money market fund, you can switch into it by telephone and then take advantage of the more convenient redemption procedures that most money market funds provide.

The Tax Impact

Remember that when you redeem shares, you have probably realized a capital gain or loss for tax purposes, and Uncle Sam is definitely looking over your shoulder. Since late 1983, banks and other mutual fund servicing agents have been required to report mutual fund redemptions to the IRS. If you forget to report your capital gains, the IRS now has an easy way to know about it. When you redeem as part of a switch from one fund to another, it is still a sale for tax purposes. In an automatic withdrawal plan, the redemptions of shares done monthly or quarterly to provide you with withdrawal checks also are redemptions like any others for tax purposes.

Money market funds, of course, are the exception. As long as a money market fund follows its stated policy of keeping its share price constant (usually at $1.00 per share), there is no gain or loss when you liquidate shares.

Chapter Nineteen

Record-keeping

Now for a brief note about record-keeping.

Mutual funds greatly simplify your record-keeping problems. But there are a few things that you should still do. When you receive the confirmation of a purchase, redemption or dividend, look at it to make sure you know what was done and that the confirmation is correct. After the end of the year, check your copy of the Form 1099 (the tax information form that the fund sends to the government) to make sure it makes sense. Also check the new form by which the fund must report all redemptions to the government, if you have redeemed shares and receive such a form. Remember, as we said earlier, that a redemption of any type is a sale of shares, which gives rise to a capital gain or loss for tax purposes.

Above all, *keep your records of share purchases,* including dividend reinvestment. Some day you are likely to sell your shares, and for tax purposes you will need to know what they originally cost. If your fund sends you a year-end statement showing all of your transactions for the calendar year, make that your prime item to file and keep.

Chapter Twenty

Taxes

The tax law gives mutual funds and their shareholders a special break. Although most funds are corporations, they escape usual corporate income taxes by *passing through* income and capital gains to their shareholders. The shareholder pays the tax, but the fund doesn't.

You owe income taxes on the income dividends and capital gains distributions you receive from a fund. If you sell your fund shares at a profit, you owe a tax on the capital gain.

If your total income dividends and capital gains distributions from a fund in a given calendar year exceed $10, the fund is required to send you a Form 1099 the following January showing these distributions as they are reported to the IRS.

The income dividends ("yield") you receive must be declared as dividend income on your tax return and are taxed as ordinary income, just like the dividends from an ordinary corporation.

The realized capital gains distributed by a mutual fund are a bit more tricky. The breakdown between long-term and short-term capital gains may not be clear to you at the time of distribution, but the breakdown should be shown clearly on your Form 1099. If the capital gains distributed are "long-term"—gains on securities that the *fund held* for long enough to meet the long-term requirement—they are reported as long-term capital gains on your income tax return, no matter how long *you* have owned your fund shares. You pay tax on only 40% of these long-term gains; in other words, your tax rate is at less than half the normal rate. But to the extent that the fund has net gains that are *short-term,* they will be reported to you as additional ordinary income and therefore fully taxable.

Mutual fund income dividends may or may not be eligible for the dividend exclusion that lets taxpayers exclude up to $100 of their total dividends from taxable income (up to $200 on a joint return). Your fund should report to you on the annual Form 1099 what part of the year's dividends are eligible for this small but pleasant tax break. A fund's dividends will be eligible ("qualifying") to the extent that the fund is passing through dividend income—and *not* eligible ("non-qualifying") to the extent that the fund is passing through interest or miscellaneous income.

For example, money market fund dividends, which derive completely from interest, are completely non-qualifying.

You should be aware that none of the usual mutual fund performance statistics make any allowance or deduction for tax liabilities, even though you will ordinarily have to pay these taxes as you go along with your mutual fund investment. You pay tax on dividends and capital gains distributions irrespective of whether or not you reinvest these distributions in additional shares.

However, from the tax standpoint a mutual fund investment is likely to be very attractive compared with most alternatives. The growth-oriented common stock funds generally aim for long-term capital gains, on which, as pointed out above, you are taxed at only 40% of normal rates. To the extent that your fund succeeds in building up the value of its shares, you enjoy an increase in asset value but owe no tax on the increase until you sell the shares. And when you do sell, the tax on any gain will again be only 40% of normal rates, assuming that you have held the shares more than the required six months.

None of the above applies to retirement plan accounts such as IRAs (Individual Retirement Accounts) and self-employed retirement plans (Keogh plans), which will be dealt with briefly in the next chapter. The law exempts those accounts from current taxes, so that they earn and compound tax-free until the money is taken out.

Chapter Twenty-one

Using the Funds for Your IRA and Keogh

In Chapter 5, we mentioned that most mutual funds offer simple arrangements for investing in an IRA (Individual Retirement Account) or self-employed retirement plan (Keogh plan).

The subject is worth returning to briefly. Prior to 1982, IRAs were only for persons who were not covered under any other retirement plan. Beginning in 1982, IRAs were opened to everyone who works for a living, whether covered by another retirement plan or not. The IRA became the first major tax break in history for the individual saver—in effect, a *tax shelter for everyone.* The law now permits anyone with *earned income* to deposit up to $2,000 a year (or up to the amount of earned income, whichever is less) into a tax-sheltered IRA and to take an income tax deduction for the amount set aside. Equally important, the IRA money earns and compounds interest or dividends tax-free until withdrawn. (See the NO-NONSENSE FINANCIAL GUIDE TO IRAS.)

In the first two years of the IRA law, Americans channeled an estimated $60 billion into these accounts. About $10 billion of this total went into mutual funds—a very respectable showing. Yet because of the blizzard of bank advertising that accompanied the new law, many people have the impression that an IRA can only be with a bank, and many have never considered a mutual fund for their IRA.

It is worth noting that mutual funds can be an excellent investment for an IRA or for a retirement plan of any type. For a younger person in particular, an IRA is a long-term investment that is ideal for common stocks and common stock funds. If you can select funds with good long-term growth rates, and let this growth compound, the long-term build-up of your money can be dramatic. For anyone who is eligible for an IRA, this is a possibility worth thinking about.

If you want to be more conservative, you can consider long-term bond funds as an IRA investment. Outside a retirement plan, the yield on bonds has the disadvantage of being fully taxable as ordinary income. But in an IRA, the yield compounds tax-free. Although we have recommended that long-term bonds be approached with caution, they can be an attractive investment for a retirement plan at times when interest rates are high and bond prices low.

The same arguments apply to self-employed retirement plans, popularly known as "Keogh" plans. Here the contribution limits were raised sharply in 1984 and now range up to $30,000 annually or more, depending on an individual's tax bracket and the type of plan chosen. If you are a businessman or professional, working as a sole proprietor or in a partnership, and can afford to make sizable contributions to a Keogh plan, your build-up for the future in a growth investment can be staggering. Even if you are a person who simply has some self-employment income on the side, in addition to a regular job, a Keogh plan makes sense for whatever contributions you can afford.

When you are ready to begin taking money out of any type of retirement plan, an automatic withdrawal plan is a simple way to provide regular cash withdrawals while keeping the balance of your plan working for you in the type of fund you prefer. If, at this point, you want to be absolutely sure of your dollars and to take no risks at all, the money market funds provide an obvious answer, and you can easily arrange to switch part or all of your plan into the money market fund of your choice.

Chapter Twenty-two

Growth and Income: The Best of Both Worlds

This is a bonus chapter. Its purpose is to leave you with an extra idea that may help you and that you may not easily learn elsewhere. It is especially important for readers who need some spendable income from their investments.

Refer back for a moment to Chapter 3. We talked about investing for growth and obtaining spendable income. These are usually talked about as requiring very different investment approaches. If you need spendable income, you will often be advised to keep at least part of your money in more conservative investments that sacrifice growth possibilities to obtain dependable interest or dividends.

But this approach carries penalties. Over the long run the best total results have been achieved by investors who invest (carefully) for *growth*. Over ten-year or fifteen-year periods, investors who have put money in the better common stock *growth* funds have done far better than investors in bonds, money market funds, or even more conservative stock funds. In the five years 1979–83 the *average* growth fund achieved a total return that worked out to *over 20% annually,* compounded. The best-performing growth funds did even better. Is it worth giving up that potential and sticking to low-growth or no-growth investments because you need perhaps 10% or 12% spendable income?

Of course, there may be more involved than your need for income. You may be happy only with an investment that gives you a dependable return every year, and you may simply be too uncomfortable with the price fluctuations of a typical growth fund.

But if you can take a long-run approach and are willing to live with price fluctuations, there's another way out. With a mutual fund you can go for growth and, in effect, *spend* part of the growth as you go along. Here's how:

Say you owned a "just average" growth fund during the years 1979–83. As stated above, this average fund would have shown a total return of about 20% annually. Let's assume that this total included dividends of 2% annually plus growth of 18%, on the average. Let's also assume that you needed a 10% *spendable* return.

To get your 10% spendable return, you could have sold 8% of your shares every year and added this to the 2% you received in cash dividends. The total value of the remaining shares would still have grown at an average rate of 10% annually—a very good rate.

One way of doing this mechanically is by setting up an automatic withdrawal plan (see Chapter 5). You instruct the fund regarding the amount of the check you want to receive monthly or quarterly, and the fund redeems just enough shares each time to provide the necessary cash. Many fund shareholders have used this arrangement with satisfaction. In many cases (depending on the market situation and the size of withdrawals) they have been able to withdraw the needed spendable money and still see some growth in the value of their remaining shares.

If you are in a high tax bracket, this approach also has a distinct tax advantage compared with investing for ordinary income or dividends. You have very little ordinary income taxable at full rates; most of your income, over the long run, will be long-term capital gains taxed at lower rates.

What are the drawbacks? First, this approach only works if you are investing for the long run. Growth funds have good years and bad years; you need to follow the approach long enough for the basic growth trend to work out. Second, you have to set yourself a reasonable schedule and stick to it. In a bad year, when the market is down and your fund may drop 10% or more in value, it may feel uncomfortable to reduce your holding an additional 6% to 10% by withdrawals; you need to have confidence that your program is reasonable, and that you will make up the "deficit" in the next good year, when your fund may be up 20% or 25%. Obviously, you need to take great care in your choice of fund. You need to apply the principles discussed in Chapter 10, watch the results carefully (Chapters 11 and 13), and don't be afraid to switch if your fund does badly for six months or a year relative to funds of the same type.

Note how perfectly mutual funds fit into this investment approach: (1) You have a very wide choice of growth funds offering different degrees of risk and managed by outstanding professionals. (2) You can invest money and take money out in relatively small amounts and with great flexibility. In some other types of investment—for example, real estate property—it may be hard to "spend" part of your growth in value without selling the whole investment or taking out an expensive loan. If you were to invest in common stocks directly, it would be relatively expensive to buy and sell in smaller amounts. (3) You can have the extra convenience of an automatic withdrawal plan.

For convenience in this type of operation, it is hard to match a good mutual fund—or a few good mutual funds. (We are certainly not suggesting that you have to limit yourself to one.)

So if you need income but want growth as well—consider the message of this chapter, choose your funds carefully, and you may well be able to enjoy the best of both worlds.

HAPPY INVESTING!!

Glossary

Adviser—See Investment Adviser.

Automatic Reinvestment—A plan by which income dividends and/or capital gains distributions are automatically applied to buy additional shares of a mutual fund.

Balanced Fund—See Chapter 7.

Bond—A long-term debt security issued by a government or corporation promising repayment of a given amount by a given date, plus interest.

Bond Fund—A mutual fund investing primarily in bonds.

Bookshares—Shares of a fund owned by an investor and recorded on the books of a fund without a certificate being issued.

Broker-Dealer—A term including several types of firms in the securities business who usually do business with the public.

Capital—Wealth invested or available for investment.

Capital Gain—The profit from sale of a security or other asset at a price above its cost.

Capital Gains Distribution—A payment by a mutual fund to its shareholders derived from capital gains realized by the fund on sales of securities in its portfolio.

Certificate—In a mutual fund, a document showing ownership of a certain number of shares.

Common Stock—A security representing a share of ownership in a corporation.

Common Stock Fund—A mutual fund investing primarily in common stocks.

Custodian—The organization (usually a bank) that holds in safe keeping the securities and other assets of a mutual fund.

Dealer—See Broker-Dealer.

Distributor—The organization that distributes the mutual fund's shares to broker-dealers and/or the public.

Diversification—For a mutual fund, the practice of spreading investments over several different securities to reduce risk.

Dividend—A share of earnings paid to a shareholder by a mutual fund or other corporation.

Dividend Reinvestment—See Automatic Reinvestment.

Dollar Cost Averaging—Investing equal amounts of money at regular intervals. (See Chapter 15.)

Ex-Dividend, Ex-Dividend Date—See Chapter 16.

Expense Ratio—See Chapter 12.

Income Dividends—Payments to mutual fund shareholders derived from interest and dividends earned by the fund on its portfolio securities.

Index Fund—A mutual fund that holds a large number of stocks selected and weighted to match the performance of a stock market index or average.

Investment Adviser—The organization that a mutual fund pays for investment advice and, usually, general business management. The adviser is usually also the sponsor and promoter of the fund.

Investment Advisory Fee—The fee paid by the fund to the adviser. (See Chapter 12.)

Investment Company—A company in which many investors pool their money for investment. Mutual funds are the most popular type.

Issued Shares—In a mutual fund, shares for which certificates are issued.

Liquid Asset Fund—A money market fund.

Liquid Investment—An investment that can be converted easily into cash, without penalty.

Load—The sales charge or commission charged on purchase of some mutual funds.

Management Fee—See Investment Advisory Fee.

Money Market Fund—A mutual fund that aims at maximum safety, liquidity, and a constant price for its shares. Its assets are invested to earn current market interest rates on the safest, short-term, highly liquid investments.

Municipal Bond—A bond issued by a state or local government. The interest is exempt from federal income tax.

Mutual Fund—See this whole book.

Net Asset Value, Net Asset Value Per Share—See Chapter 9.

No-load Fund—A mutual fund that sells its shares at net asset value, without any commission.

Offering Price—See Chapter 13.

Open-end Investment Company—A mutual fund. Technically called "open-end" because the fund stands ready to sell new shares to investors or to buy back shares submitted for redemption.

Portfolio—The total list of securities owned by a mutual fund or by any investor.

Portfolio Manager—An individual who makes decisions regarding buying, selling, or holding securities for an investment organization.

Principal—The capital or main body of an investment, as distinguished from the income earned on it.

Prospectus—The official document describing a mutual fund and offering its shares for sale. See Chapter 12.

Redemption—The procedure by which a mutual fund buys back shares from shareholders on demand.

Redemption Price—See Chapters 9 and 18.

SEC—the U.S. Securities and Exchange Commission: The federal agency charged with regulating securities markets and the investment industry (including mutual funds).

Security—General term meaning stocks, bonds and other investment instruments.

Shareholder Servicing Agent—The bank or other organization that maintains a fund's shareholder records and processes shareholder transactions.

Stock—A security representing an ownership interest in a corporation.

Transfer Agent—See Shareholder Servicing Agent.

Underwriter or Principal Underwriter—See Distributor.

Unissued Shares—In a mutual fund, this term refers to book shares. (See Bookshares.)

Withdrawal Plan—A plan by which a mutual fund shareholder receives regular periodic checks (usually monthly or quarterly) from his or her investment. The checks are derived from accumulated dividends or capital gains distributions and/or automatic redemptions of shares.

Yield—The return on an investment. In securities, the dividends or interest received, usually expressed as a percentage of the value of the investment.

TABLE A

Best Performing Mutual Funds—10 Years—12/31/73–12/31/83

Listed by Objective

All funds have net assets of more than $100 million

Name	Total % Gain	$1,000 Would Have Become	Annual Growth Rate	Load/ No-load	Minimum Initial Investment	Toll-free Telephone Number
AGGRESSIVE GROWTH FUNDS						
Twentieth Century Growth Investors	930.0%	$10,300	26.3%	no-load	no minimum	no toll-free number 816-531-5575
American Capital Pace	913.4%	$10,134	26.1%	load	$500	800-231-3638
American Capital Comstock	773.4%	$8,734	24.2%	load	$500	800-231-3638
Value Line Leveraged Growth	723.8%	$8,238	23.5%	no-load	$250	800-223-0818
American Capital Venture	694.4%	$7,944	23.0%	load	$500	800-231-3638
Seligman Capital Fund	564.8%	$6,648	20.9%	load	no minimum	800-221-2450
44 Wall Street Fund	544.0%	$6,440	20.5%	no-load	$1,000	800-221-7836
Weingarten Equity Fund	471.8%	$5,718	19.0%	no-load	$1,000	no toll-free number 212-557-8787
Janus Fund	447.9%	$5,479	18.5%	no-load	$1,000	800-525-3713
Constellation Growth Fund	438.3%	$5,383	18.3%	no-load	$1,000	no toll-free number 212-557-8787
GROWTH FUNDS						
Fidelity Magellan Fund	1224.7%	$13,247	29.5%	load	$1,000	800-225-6190
Lindner Fund	1038.4%	$11,384	27.5%	no-load	$2,000	no toll-free number 314-727-5305
Oppenheimer Special Fund	1016.3%	$11,163	27.3%	load	$1,000	800-525-7048
Evergreen Fund	980.9%	$10,809	26.9%	no-load	$1,500	800-635-0003
Twentieth Century Select Investors	883.5%	$9,835	25.7%	no-load	no minimum	no toll-free number 816-531-5575
Pennsylvania Mutual Fund	723.2%	$8,232	23.5%	no-load	$2,000	800-221-4268

TABLE A (*Continued*)

Name	Total % Gain	$1,000 Would Have Become	Annual Growth Rate	Load/ No-load	Minimum Initial Investment	Toll-free Telephone Number
GROWTH FUNDS						
Fidelity Destiny Fund	694.6%	$7,946	23.0%	load	$50	800-225-6190
Value Line Special Situations Fund	588.5%	$6,885	21.3%	no-load	$250	800-223-0818
AMCAP Fund	542.6%	$6,426	20.4%	load	$1,000	800-421-9900
Growth Fund of America	519.7%	$6,197	20.0%	load	$1,000	800-421-9900
GROWTH AND INCOME FUNDS						
Mutual Shares Corporation	793.3%	$8,933	24.5%	no-load	$1,000	800-221-7864
Pioneer II Fund	683.1%	$7,831	22.9%	load	$250	800-225-6292
Windsor Fund	474.6%	$5,746	19.1%	no-load	$500	800-523-7025
Value Line Fund	433.8%	$5,338	18.2%	no-load	$250	800-223-0818
FPA Paramount Fund	394.8%	$4,948	17.3%	load	$1,500	800-421-4374
Guardian Mutual Fund	383.2%	$4,832	17.1%	no-load	$200	800-367-0770
American Mutual Fund	362.3%	$4,623	16.5%	load	$250	800-421-9900
American Capital Harbor Fund	352.5%	$4,525	16.3%	load	$500	800-231-3638
Delaware Fund	334.2%	$4,342	15.8%	load	$25	800-523-1918
Washington Mutual Investors	322.6%	$4,226	15.5%	load	$250	800-421-9900
EQUITY INCOME FUNDS						
Fidelity Equity-Income Fund	546.4%	$6,464	20.5%	load	$1,000	800-225-6190
Oppenheimer Equity Income Fund	430.0%	$5,300	18.1%	load	$250	800-525-7048
Value Line Income Fund	370.9%	$4,709	16.8%	no-load	$250	800-223-0818

TABLE A (*Continued*)

Name	Total % Gain	$1,000 Would Have Become	Annual Growth Rate	Load/ No-load	Minimum Initial Investment	Toll-free Telephone Number
EQUITY INCOME FUNDS						
Financial Industrial Income Fund	333.0%	$4,330	15.8%	load	$1,000	800-525-9831
Decatur Income Fund	332.3%	$4,323	15.8%	load	$25	800-523-1918
National Total Return Fund	329.4%	$4,294	15.7%	load	$250	800-223-7757
Fidelity Puritan Fund	298.0%	$3,980	14.8%	no-load	$1,000	800-225-6190
Income Fund of America	279.7%	$3,797	14.3%	load	$1,000	800-421-9900
National Income Fund	271.8%	$3,718	14.0%	load	$250	800-223-7757
United Income Fund	164.7%	$2,647	10.2%	load	$500	800-283-4000
BALANCED FUNDS						
Kemper Total Return Fund	388.4%	$4,884	17.2%	load	$1,000	800-621-1048
Eaton Vance Investors Fund	215.5%	$3,155	12.2%	load	$20	800-225-6206
Axe-Houghton Fund B	183.3%	$2,833	11.0%	load	$1,000	800-431-1030
Wellington Fund	181.8%	$2,818	10.9%	no-load	$500	800-523-7025
American Balanced Fund	175.6%	$2,756	10.7%	load	$500	800-421-9900
SPECIALIZED FUNDS						
Templeton Growth Fund (International)	497.7%	$5,977	19.6%	load	$500	800-237-0738
International Investors (Gold)	427.3%	$5,273	18.1%	load	$1,000	800-221-2220
New Perspective Fund (International)	311.6%	$4,116	15.2%	load	$250	800-421-9900
Oppenheimer A.I.M. Fund (International)	267.9%	$3,679	13.9%	load	$250	800-525-7048
Energy Fund (Natural Resources)	263.8%	$3,638	13.8%	no-load	$250	800-367-0770

TABLE B

BEST PERFORMING BOND FUNDS—10 YEARS—12/31/73–12/31/83

All funds have net assets of more than $100 million

Name	Total % Gain	$1000 Would Have Become	Annual Growth Rate	Load/ No-load	Minimum Initial Investment	Toll-free Telephone Number
Lord Abbett Bond Debenture Fund	224.1%	$3,241	12.5%	load	$1,000	800-223-4224
First Investors Fund for Income	201.4%	$3,014	11.7%	load	$200	no toll-free number 212-825-7900
Keystone B-4	198.6%	$2,986	11.6%	no-load	$250	800-225-1587
IDS Bond Fund	165.9%	$2,659	10.3%	load	$2,000	800-437-4332
Bond Fund of America	145.4%	$2,454	9.4%	load	$1,000	800-421-9900
Investors Selective Fund	138.5%	$2,385	9.1%	load	$2,000	800-328-8300
Mass. Financial Bond Fund	138.3%	$2,383	9.1%	load	no minimum	no toll-free number 617-423-3500
T. Rowe Price New Income Fund	131.9%	$2,319	8.8%	no-load	$1,000	800-638-5660
Putnam Income Fund	125.0%	$2,250	8.4%	load	$500	800-354-4000
Northeast Investors Trust	122.8%	$2,228	8.3%	no-load	$500	800-225-6704

Note: This was a period of generally declining bond prices, which had an adverse effect on the total performance of most bond funds.

TABLE C

Best Performing Tax-exempt Bond Funds—5 Years—12/31/78-12/31/83
All funds have net assets of more than $100 million

Name	Total % Gain	$1000 Would Have Become	Annual Growth Rate	Load/ No-load	Minimum Initial Investment	Toll-free Telephone Number
Putnam Tax Exempt Income Fund	56.9%	$1,569	9.4%	load	$500	800-354-4000
MFS Managed Municipal Bond Trust	54.6%	$1,546	9.1%	load	no minimum	no toll-free number 617-423-3500
Vanguard Municipal Bond Fund—Short Term	38.3%	$1,383	6.7%	no-load	$3,000	800-523-7025
T. Rowe Price Tax-Free Income Fund	34.5%	$1,345	6.1%	no-load	$1,000	800-638-5660
Scudder Managed Municipal Bonds	29.6%	$1,296	5.3%	no-load	$1,000	800-225-2470
First Investors Tax Exempt Fund	28.5%	$1,285	5.1%	load	$1,000	no toll-free number 212-825-7900
SteinRoe Tax-Exempt Bond Fund	28.0%	$1,280	5.1%	no-load	$2,500	800-621-0320
Fidelity High Yield Municipals	27.4%	$1,274	5.0%	no-load	$2,500	800-225-6190
Keystone Tax-Free Fund	27.3%	$1,273	4.9%	load	$250	800-225-1587
Fidelity Limited Term Municipals	26.1%	$1,261	4.7%	no-load	$2,500	800-225-6190

Note: This was a period of generally declining bond prices, which had an adverse affect on the total performance of most bond funds.

TABLE D
Selected Major No-load Mutual Fund Groups

Group Name	Toll-free Telephone Number
Alliance Capital Management Corporation (subsidiary of Donaldson, Lufkin & Jenrette)	800-221-9513
The Dreyfus Corporation	800-645-6561
Fidelity Management & Research Co.	800-225-6190
Financial Programs Inc.	800-525-9831
Lehman Management Co., Inc.	800-221-5350
Neuberger & Berman Management	800-367-0770
T. Rowe Price Associates, Inc.	800-638-5660
Scudder, Stevens & Clark	800-225-2470
Stein, Roe & Farnham	800-621-0320
Value Line Group (Arnold Bernhard & Co.)	800-223-0818
Vanguard Group	800-523-7025

Arnold Corrigan, noted financial expert, is a senior officer of a large New York investment advisory firm. He holds bachelor's and master's degrees in economics from Harvard and has written for *Barron's* and other financial publications. He is the author of *How Your IRA Can Make You a Millionaire.*

Phyllis C. Kaufman is an entertainment lawyer and theatrical producer with degrees from Brandeis and Temple universities. Also a marketing and public relations consultant, she hopes that the NO-NONSENSE FINANCIAL GUIDES will help others conquer their "fear of finance."